IT'S
All
GOOD

*A transformational workbook
for the undecided student in you.*

Karl Hutchings Jr.

Editors: Kathy Kinney and Paul Baker
Book Cover Artist: Rachael Noxon

ISBN 978-0-615-26931-3

Pegasus Publishing

Table of Contents

Introduction/Acknowledgements...6

How to Use This Book...7

Lesson 1
Characteristics of Undecided Students..................................10
     Give Yourself a Break
     Undecided Students are Typically Humanitarians
     The "Humanitarian Paradox"
     It's All in the Thinking

Lesson 2
Agreements of *Shoulds*...14
     Stage 1
     Agreements of Shoulds
     The Should-Fear Connection
     Fear of Speaking Up/Not Being Understood
     What Do You Want?
     The Positive Side of Difficulties
     Difficulties Lead to Virtues

Lesson 3
Transforming the Way You Think...19
     Powerless Agreements – Thinking As a Victim
     Victim Agreement Statements
     Change your Agreements
     Powerless Thinking
     Prosperous vs. Scarcity Thinking
     Going for Broke
     Stage 2: A Path to Changing Your Should Agreements and The Way You Think

Lesson 4

Embracing Creative Consciousness…………………………...……………25

Stage 3

Who Am I?

The Law of Attraction

Small Steps

We Create Our Future

The Authentic Self is Powerful

Mastering Faith is the Power of Creating

Power of Attention

Power of Thoughts

Dualities of Right and Wrong

Lesson 5

Joy Requires Truth……………………………………..……………....32

Extreme Thinking Restricts Joy

Absolute Truth Separates Us

The Truth: Life Wants to Bring Us Joy

Authentic Self Lives in Joy and Love

True Gifts

Lesson 6

Applying Concepts to Reality: Choosing a Career Path…....……………36

Career Path Connection

Change is Painful

Purposeful Education

Interpersonal Communication Must be Strengthened

Get Started

Preparedness Calms the Storms

Being Prepared Requires Faith

Lesson 7

Self-Respect in Personal Relationships……………………..………42

WORKSHEETS 1 through 12…………………………………………...………..45

Worksheet 1:   *List of Shoulds*
Worksheet 2:   *List of Fears*
Worksheet 3:   *List of Wants*
Worksheet 4:   *List of Difficulties*
Worksheet 5:   *List of Frustrations*
Worksheet 6:   *Gratitude List*
Worksheet 7:   *List of Memories*
Worksheet 8:   *Beliefs Springing from Memories*
Worksheet 9:   *Thoughts & Beliefs*
Worksheet 10:   *The Cycle of Life Circle*
Worksheet 11:   *Creating a New Cycle of Life*
Worksheet 12:   *Write Your Script/Autobiography*
                    Sample Script/Autobiography

INTRODUCTION/ACKNOWLEDGEMENT

Karl Hutchings Jr. has been a member of the staff at a western state college since 1984. He spent nine of those years in college recruiting and the past fourteen years as Director of Cooperative Education (Co-op). Co-op is a program designed to give college students credit for working in a field related to their major. Shortly after his first year as Director of Co-op, he realized that many students felt compelled to "make-up" their declaration of a major in order to receive credit. The students needed the credits to get the funding to stay in school. In order to address this problem, working in collaboration with key school administrators, Karl spearheaded the development of the General Co-op program which is designed to provide a path for those students with an undecided major rather than forcing them into a premature decision. The primary purpose of the General Co-op is to establish a safe place for undecided students who are not quite ready to make a decision about a major or a career path. By providing students a sense of acceptance, the General Co-op program empowers students to explore a variety of work and career options.

Students who have not declared a college major are referred to as "undecided" in the world of academics. It was soon apparent to Karl that a high percentage of students were undecided about their major. In many cases, they were enrolled in college because their parents and/or "society" had convinced them that they "should" go to college, and that college was the best way to get a good paying job and become successful. Although a college degree is a laudable goal, it is important that students see the value themselves, rather than enrolling to please others.

Years of working with and counseling undecided students has given Karl an unprecedented insight into where undecided students are in their lives and what kind of guidance they need. This book reflects the culmination of many years of theory and practice Karl has used in counseling undecided students. In addition to his own experiences, Karl relied on the insight of others in writing this book, especially the students who took the time to read early versions of this book and provided invaluable feedback. Karl also thanks his colleagues for their support. Special thanks to Kathy Kinney and Paul Baker, a close friend and adviser and publishing agent, for encouragement along the way as well as editing thoughts and words and spending unending hours discussing and refining the concepts of this book.

If you would like to contact Karl, he can be reached via email at hutching@dixie.edu.

HOW TO USE THIS BOOK

The information contained in these pages is intended to aid undecided students as well as faculty, advisors, parents and fellow students in their interaction with undecided students. The information and worksheets are designed to guide undecided students in self-reflection that will lead to discoveries. It is those discoveries that are valuable for making decisions about a college major and a career path. Along the way, the book identifies 3 progressive Stages that undecided students tend to move through. Most are stuck in Stage 1. This book and worksheets, coupled with a student's active and focused participation, shows the way to work out of Stage 1 and across Stage 2 with the ultimate goal of living a life in Stage 3 where, for example, decisions come easier because they spring from your authentic self.

Although this book is focused on students (primarily high school and college students) and the choices they face, it is also applicable to life choices. In fact, it is hard to separate the two, and there are a number of places in this book where concepts and ideas ebb and flow from educational major/career paths to living the life you want. **The book addresses both and often moves from showing you how to live a life you want and/or picking a major and a career path. As the reader, try to be patient in grasping the stated concepts (you may not "get it" the first time around) and also be patient in discovering the interrelationship of the two.**

Also, the book may be viewed by some as being "outside" the traditional box of a career guide in that some of the concepts discussed in the book may seem either foreign or perhaps "odd" or too "new age." The workbook does borrow from many philosophies and disciplines (some ancient, some contemporary and some between the two), but the power of this book is bringing it all together in a useful, practical way which could only be accomplished through many years of working with undecided students. The concepts in this book are consistent with most religious or spiritual beliefs.

Despite rigorous attempts to organize these materials in a logical way, I leaned to the side of sharing as many concepts and ideas helpful to the topic with the understanding that tangents sometimes need to supersede organization in certain sections. You will find the worksheets very helpful in pulling it all together.

If you open your mind and spend time reading these words and working through the worksheets, you will find that you'll start walking down a new path where you live your highest potential of creativity, joy, abundance, gratitude and love, not just in school or at work but in all aspects of your life. The energy, rigor and attention you give to the instruction in this book, along with incorporating the information into your experience behavioral habits, will determine the time it will take for you to start living the life you have always wanted.

Working through the exercises in this book will require support from someone who is willing to understand the way undecided students think. This person (or group) will have to respect others. *Since undecided students tend to have difficulty trusting others, they may not feel safe to disclose the information in their assignments.* Therefore, the students should only disclose the things they feel safe in talking about. Eventually, the students will find that the methodology used to resolve *all* issues will be the same and can work on their more sensitive issues when they find the right, safe helper.

Although it is difficult to summarize this book in a few lines, let me just say that if you put your heart and soul into this book and the assignments, you will be able to answer three essential questions that will fundamentally alter your view on life and consequently will help in choosing a major and career path.

First, you will be able to see *"Who YOU are."* Second you will know *"What YOU really want."* And third you will understand *"What steps YOU need to take to get there."* You'll understand the importance of these questions as you move through the book. In fact, the last worksheet walks you through the process of writing your own life script where you take the answers to these questions and transform them into an action-oriented life plan.

Completing the worksheets is critical to getting the most out of this book. Just reading the book will help you to some extent, but to truly make a difference in your life, you are encouraged to complete every assignment with rigor and focused intention. The first step is to understand the typical "make-up" of an undecided student. You will probably see that you have many of these same traits. It is through this process that you will start discovering "Who YOU really are" and uncovering the steps you can take in improving your academic experience, career and life.

Consider this book a journey comprised of 7 lessons followed by 12 worksheets. Take your time. Go at your own pace. There is no finish line. Rather, it's an ongoing journey. And it's YOUR journey. Then you will be ready to create life your way. So enjoy!

Follow these steps to use this book most effectively:

1. *Read the text.*
2. *Complete all the worksheets.*
3. *Re-read the text with the understanding that you gained by doing the worksheets.*

I also want to share that I struggled with the title of this book. The title is simply a title and really insignificant to the concepts contained inside; on the other hand, it does relay in three words a powerful theme that runs throughout this book. Hopefully you'll see it. And don't be fooled, it's NOT all good without work, effort and understanding; but if you put into practice the concepts discussed in this book and the worksheets, you have the power to understand and manifest the simple fact that "it" really is all good. Read on and see if you agree.

LESSON 1
Characteristics of Undecided Students

There comes a point in college when undecided students must declare a major. This is usually preceded by selecting a career path. Yet, undecided students find this choice to be so important they freeze and postpone it until the last possible moment. This puts undecided students in a challenging place. They typically feel pressure by parents, family, friends and academic advisors to finally answer the question, ***"What do you want to be when you grow up?"*** ***This really is not a useful question although it is the question undecided students are often posed!*** Although the question typically is asked with good intentions, it is a question that creates more pressure rather than relieving it. The better question to ask is: "***What service or commodity do you want to create that is in harmony with your authentic self and from which the world would benefit***?" Just altering one question moves the undecided student from a place of pressure to a place of possibilities.

Being open to new ideas is often difficult for undecided students. They have done such a perfect job of developing a play-it-safe game plan that they often resist new ideas, methods or experiences at which they could fail. Therefore, it can be a slow process of development from a dependency on what others think to breaking free. Of course, most undecided students won't see this at first because they lost sight of who they are at an early age when they decided to play it safe. But this old way of thinking can be transformed. It just requires some work to bring back that fearless mindset where anything is possible.

Give Yourself a Break

If you are an undecided student, you are not alone. And there is nothing "wrong" with you. To be undecided is as "normal" as being "decided." In fact, as will be discussed, "undecided" students tend to possess many unique and virtuous characteristics. So give yourself a break! *Many* students in college take general education courses to get them out of the way before declaring a major. Filling in with an elective or two of exploratory classes to test out a major is common. This is actually an effective way to continue to make progress toward a degree without committing to a major. Yes, perhaps it is a path filled with more uncertainty, yet it is an effective path for that very reason. This path is something to embrace rather than fear. Just understanding this distinction hopefully gives you some comfort.

Undecided students tend to be too hard on themselves when it comes to declaring a major. It may appear that all their friends have been able to discern what to do with their lives. *This can lead undecided students to think of themselves as less capable or less intelligent or less brave. In fact, undecided students are none of these things.*

Another way to "give yourself a break" is to understand that declaring a major and taking steps towards a career path are just that: "steps." Although these decisions should not be taken lightly – and indeed this book is all about helping you make those steps – if you embrace the notion that steps you take now may lead to paths and outcomes that you did not necessarily envision when you started out, you will find that decisions become easier as fear of making the "wrong" choice falls away.

Undecided Students are Typically Humanitarians

Undecided students are really quite amazing and unique. And it's not by chance. You were made that way by your early life experiences which developed the thoughts and beliefs that you could make everyone happy. *You have developed highly sensitive awareness to what others are thinking and feeling and you feel responsible to make this world a perfect place.* Your intentions are to save everyone, everything and perhaps every animal. *You have compassion for others sometimes to the extent that your feelings overwhelm you.* See, you really are amazing and unique. And yes, you have a lot of work to do to help change the world into a better place.

Undecided students generally have complex personalities and, in many cases, have lived a life filled with challenges, whether real or perceived. The challenges they have faced and lived through could be detrimental, but for the humanitarian (people who genuinely and naturally care about other people), these experiences tend to positively impact their lives even if they may not be conscious of this positive impact. They have come out of the other side of these challenges with a number of admirable qualities. For instance, they often find themselves wanting to make everyone happy, healthy and safe. *They have attributes of sensitivity, compassion, service, gentleness, intuition, support and grace.* In return, they have built self worth.

The "Humanitarian Paradox"

The irony is that *humanitarians often don't know what their own dreams are, but they think they want to help everyone else attain theirs. To understand this paradox is to solve it so you can create your own dreams without abandoning your humanitarian principles.*

There is one prominent dilemma undecided students face (as do humanitarians generally): because you think you are responsible for everyone else's happiness, you can find a hundred reasons why you don't deserve to be happy or to go after your own dreams. You may think that is selfish. And if you are to save the world from pain, then you don't want to create any pain for others. So you find yourself pleasing everyone else, and you have created a belief that this is your purpose in life. And by this purpose, you have played it safe so you will never offend or cause any problems. It need not be this way.

Again, the paradox is: When you play it safe, you lose. When you risk losing, you win. Then you will find your authentic self again. Therefore you will have *to think in courage to risk, in freedom to make mistakes, and in flexibility to explore* in order to use all of your wonderful talents that you developed by experiencing conflicts and challenges. You really are the luckiest people because you possess the finest virtues. Enjoy this workbook and challenge yourself to be authentic every day in every way. *Now, let's discover how you have strayed from your authentic self and what steps must be taken to return.*

This paradox is not so easy to solve. It takes work. Undecided students want to save the world. OK, what's wrong with that? Absolutely nothing. But too often, this desire may not stem from the student's true humanitarian self, but rather the student is really trying to save themselves from false fears: the fear of failure, the fear of not being good enough and the fear of not measuring up. Unable to conquer their own fears, they grab on to the notion of helping others. Removing fear will return them to their authentic self. Their calling will then be to share the methodology or message with others so they can do the same. In this environment, the fear disappears and the student's true humanitarian self is uncovered.

When undecided students understand who they are and overcome the false fears that have imprisoned their experience and their ability to communicate, then their major (or calling) in life rises to the surface. This new perspective empowers them to envision a career in law, medicine, education, business, philosophy, computers or any other degree. *And their intentions will change from playing it safe in these fields to breaking new boundaries in these fields*. For example, it is one thing to say, "Well, I guess I will go to law school…becoming a lawyer is a good way to make money" versus an empowered view that says "I have a passion for the law and I want to explore all the knowledge it holds." Students with this latter viewpoint will be the ones who challenge traditions, knock down walls and create new possibilities. *They will reject rote thinking and, instead, stand for principles and virtues not in self righteousness but in an awareness for the good of all.* This is not an easy place to reach, but absolutely satisfying when it is. As will be discussed later, it is in this place that principles will be in harmony with authentic self.

It's All in the Thinking

As will be discussed more fully in later lessons, undecided students are in need of creating a new way of thinking. They will have to understand that as a child their experiences caused them to think a certain way; their thoughts created a belief or conclusion. *And their conclusions have been creating thoughts, which dictate their experiences and behavior as adults.*

By removing the thoughts of fear and conquering life's difficulties of communication, undecided students, once they wake up, will have a powerful impact on society. Humanitarians, free of fear, have the qualities to lead this generation into a life of peace, power and prosperity and into a world free of strife and war. In this way, undecided students are students we should embrace as opposed to pressuring them into paths that are not true to their authentic selves.

Now, let's move to Lesson 2 and understand how undecided students unintentionally find themselves in a state of fear where their true selves have been buried.

LESSON 2
The Agreement of *Shoulds*

◘ *Pause here and complete WORKSHEET 1.*

<u>Agreements of Shoulds</u>

(Refer to WORKSHEET 1 and what you have written in your list of SHOULDS as you read this section.)

Most undecided students are in Stage 1 of life. They are continuing to be compliant and to do what authority figures have been telling them to do, thinking what they have been told to think, and becoming what they have been told to become and are fearful of not measuring up to rules, standards and expectations. In this Stage, undecided students feel their sole purpose is to meet the obligations and expectations that have been demanded of them for the past 18+ years of their lives. The expectations come from family, friends, teachers, spiritual leaders, peers and a multitude of other sources. Because students accept these expectations and agree to make them their own, these expectations are called *Agreements of Shoulds*. It is worth mentioning again that these expectations that others put on you may often be well-intentioned and indeed may lead to the right path for you. Listen to what others say, but ultimately *do* what your true, inner self leads you to do. This is the distinction between "shoulds" and "wants."

The word *should* is perhaps the most destructive word in the English language. **The word "should" carriers with it the implication that you will always be wrong if you don't do what you should.** Undecided students have a long list of *shoulds*. Every *should* expectations can create a fear of not living up to the *should*. A very high percentage of undecided students can be profiled as students in Stage 1. Students in Stage 1 exhibit the following behaviors, among others:

- If they cannot be proficient, they will not even try.
- They procrastinate until the last minute to give justification for not doing a perfect job.
- They *focus on what they are not doing right*, how they are not meeting expectations, how they might mess up and/or how they are not doing what they *should*.

These are the behaviors of perfectionism and lead students to create their most significant fear: The fear of failure or fear of making a mistake or the fear of not pleasing others. Because of this fear, students in Stage 1 tend to be undecided students. *They are afraid to make any choice because it may be the wrong choice.* The good news is that it need not be this way, and you control the way out.

◘ *Pause here and complete WORKSHEET 2.*

<u>The Should-Fear Connection</u>

(Refer to WORKSHEET 2 and what you have written in your list of FEARS as you read this.)

Every should is fear-based. It is the fear of not measuring up or not accomplishing your *shoulds*. Fears are often connected to duality judgment, which means things are either right or wrong without room for variance. To be successful, students must let go of the judgment of right or wrong associated with duality which then makes room for growth. *When the only options are right or wrong, students naturally get stuck in indecision.*

Indecision plagues undecided students with fear because they do not feel safe to make a mistake, to fail, to lose or to be wrong. The agreement inherent in the indecision associated with Stage 1 is *if you are afraid to fail, you cannot succeed*. Therefore, indecision interferes with students' growth, restricts their exploration and imprisons their experience. The feeling of not being good enough is what I call *life's only temptation*. It leads students to settle, to quit or to give up. The *fear of not being good enough leads to every dysfunction the world has ever known.* It causes us all to settle into what the American author Henry David Thoreau calls a life of "quiet desperation" in which we never reach our highest potential despite a desperate desire to reach it. It is also a self-fulfilling prophecy. If you live in fear, it results in failure which further reinforces the original fear.

Fear of Speaking Up/Not Being Understood

Fear creates one of the highest challenges most undecided students face: *developing appropriate interpersonal communications.* For example, fear of speaking up to disagree, or to agree for that matter, is a significant difficulty. Since undecided students have felt wrong most of the time, *they rarely feel safe enough to communicate thoughts and feelings because of the lack of validation from authority figures in the past.* Undecided students also often feel that even when they do speak up, they are not heard or understood. Fear of speaking up (and the fear of being misunderstood) causes undecided students to become frustrated because their *self-worth is based mainly on what others think.* They do not want to disappoint anyone or disappoint themselves. *Therefore, their unintended focus is on frustrations.*

The fear of speaking up and not being understood creates a passive or a passive-aggressive style in the undecided student's efforts to communicate. In addition, the fear of speaking up creates a bigger problem than that of speaking up itself. When undecided students try to please everyone to gain approval, they get mad at themselves. *Their inner communication becomes full of bitterness, anger and resentment because of the dishonesty in their interpersonal communication.* It causes them to say "yes" when they don't feel they have the right to say "no." *It causes them to play it safe so they will never be wrong.*

Behind this communication style is the agreement *"I always need to be right."* Some call this being stubborn. Others may define it as being shy. The agreement came from an experience of *inconsistencies from authority figures with absolute power*. This is exhibited in ways such as, the rules of one parent being different from the other, or the first grade teacher being different from subsequent teachers. What was right for one was wrong for the other. Since the agreement is "I always have to be right" experiences such as the ones mentioned make students feel stupid, wrong or inadequate. *Students become so careful in this agreement that they lose their authentic selves along the way and life quickly becomes difficult.*

You have the ability to break this cycle and, even more importantly, turn the cycle completely around to create a self-fulfilling prophecy of success. Instead of a fear-based mindset, you live in a confident, courageous state-of-mind; this in turn leads to success which further reinforces your confidence and courage. This switch is very powerful – indeed almost all people who are highly effective, happy and find joy in life have confidence and courage. They *view failure as a step to success*, not something to be feared but rather an important part of reaching their highest potential.

Thoughts that dominate students' minds become their reality. When they are not living up to their list of shoulds, the thoughts that dominate their minds are that of failure, scarcity, inadequacy, disappointment, and frustration. As those thoughts persist, the students continue to believe they are not good enough. If undecided students can change thought patterns to recognize and ***focus on what they are doing right rather than focusing on what they should be doing, then they can reclaim their authentic selves and change their destiny.*** The students can direct their lives down a path that they chose to create and move away from the path of feeling like a victim of circumstances.

◘ ***Pause here and complete WORKSHEET 3.***

What Do You Want?

(Refer to WORKSHEET 3 and what you have written in your list of WANTS as you read this section.)

What students write in the *WANTS* column is significant. Most undecided students will include travel to experience different cultures and to explore life in a different way. In other words, they want ***freedom from their personal list of shoulds.*** Rarely will they match their *wants* list to their *shoulds* list. The conflict in their lists causes an even greater conflict in their minds. It is important to live life by the values represented by the list of *WANTS*. ***Freedom, service, support, trust, power, respect, prosperity, joy, peace, flexibility and courage typically are the main values of those who are undecided.*** Often these values represent the opposite of how they have been living. ***Living in the opposite of what you want creates many difficulties and a state of disharmony.***

◘ ***Pause here and complete WORKSHEET 4.***

The Positive Side of Difficulties

(Refer to WORKSHEET 4 and what you have written in your list of DIFFICULTIES as you read this section.)

All of life's experiences lead to ***agreements that either enhance or restrict lives***. Culture, parents, teachers, political and religious beliefs all have an impact on who we are and the agreements we make. ***The difficulties people go through build strength, courage and confidence, if they make it through the difficulty successfully***. On the other hand, if the person does not deal with the difficulty or move through it, the difficulty creates a weakness that can possibly haunt them for the rest of their lives.

Difficulties Lead to Virtues

Students cannot avoid difficulties; however, it is important to consider what is learned and gained through life's difficulties. Those who have accepted the agreement "I always have to be right" want to be saved from the pain of not being in harmony with their authentic selves. Yet there is something to be gained from the disharmony difficulties present. While working through the difficulty, many virtues are being developed. ***Sensitivity being the first***. In order to not cause further feelings of inadequacy, a sensitivity and intuition for others is built. This includes being able to sense someone's mood or determine when and how to approach someone without offending. This difficulty helps students become *caretakers* and creates a desire to save others from pain. They gain the virtues of gentleness, kindness, responsibility and service. **These are divine virtues.**

However, in many cases gaining these virtues through difficulty stems not from your authentic self, but rather from an effort to be good enough. Sometimes actions are taken to stave off guilt, to be right or to gain approval from others. ***The motivation comes from the fallen state of inadequacy rather than from having the natural flow of abundance***. Try to understand that although you may have amazing attributes and virtues, what determines whether you are in harmony depends on the source causing those attributes and virtues. People in harmony chose their attributes and virtues while people in disharmony take on these virtues because of "agreements of should" – often unknowingly. The result is a feeling of being a powerless victim. These feelings come from thought, and it is only through transforming the way you think that you will be able to move from a sense of powerlessness to empowerment. Lesson 3 suggests a path to transforming the way you think.

LESSON 3
Transforming the Way you Think

◘ *Pause here and complete WORKSHEET 5.*

Powerless Agreements – Thinking As a Victim

(Refer to WORKSHEET 5 and what you have written in your list of FRUSTRATIONS as you read this section. You will see that your powerless concepts are causing frustrations and indecision.)

A significant and prevalent false agreement is: I am a victim. ***Being a victim is the opposite of the nature of the authentic self.*** Often we learn to be a victim from those in authority when we are children in Stage 1. This is especially true if those in authority were unkind or cruel. ***We were blamed for things we had no control over.*** Things like "You hurt my feelings" or "Look what you made me do." No wonder you feel responsible for pleasing everyone. Undecided students have a long list of agreements that keep them locked into being a powerless victim. Go down the list of "Vice Agreement Statements" on the next page and see how many you find yourself thinking or speaking.

Victim Agreement Statements

Do you find yourself thinking or speaking any of these victim agreement statements?

1. Can you believe they did that to me?
2. It is his\her fault.
3. We are just too different to get along.
4. I want them to admit they are wrong.
5. If he/she loved me, he/she wouldn't do that.
6. I am sick and tired of that.
7. I don't have enough time, money, love, etc.
8. I am so busy. I am overwhelmed.
9. I'm just that way because…
10. I don't have the right to speak up for what I want.
11. Everyone else comes before me.
12. After all I have done for her/him.
13. When you do that, it drives me crazy.
14. I have worked 2 jobs to support you.
15. My boss doesn't like me.
16. I was late because…
17. You make me so mad, sad, frustrated etc.
18. If it's not one thing it's another.
19. He/she made me do this.
20. You don't know how hard I have tried.
21. It wasn't my idea.
22. I never can finish my work.
23. Nobody loves me.
24. They need to be taught a lesson.
25. What did I do to deserve this?
26. I deserve more because I sacrifice.
27. I'll try to get it done.

◘ *Pause here and complete WORKSHEET 6.*

Change your Agreements

(Refer to WORKSHEET 6 and what you have written in your GRATITUDE list as you read this section. It will demonstrate that gratitude is a powerful state of mind.)

Statements like those in the list above demonstrate the powerless thinking that undecided students unconsciously embrace. ***Like a dark cloud, these agreements hide the authentic self, the powerful self, the co-creator self that lies underneath a thick layer of "should agreements" that lead to "victim thinking."*** Undecided students must work hard to peel off one victim agreement after another. However, the result will be worth the effort.

(Refer to WORKSHEETS 7, 8, and 9 to discover your negative or victim agreements and determine the source of those agreements.)

You peel off and put aside your victim agreements and move from "shoulds" to "wants" by changing all victim agreements to positive agreements. (You will be asked to do this when you write your script in WORKSHEET 12.)

The methodology used to attain the life you want can never be achieved by strife or negativity, which is a form of scarcity or not being good enough. *Human thoughts have a vibration, positive and negative vibrations. Only through positive thought vibrations can we attain personal power and confidence.* Such thoughts require positive blueprints or positive agreements. ***Students can change their reality if they can change their minds regarding blueprints and agreements***.

Another paradox in the world of undecided students in Stage 1 is hating to be told what to do, yet hating to decide on their own. *It seems they rarely feel they get what they want*. And how could they? *Most of what they are doing is for someone else's approval or acceptance*. This kind of life is shallow, mundane, stressful, fearful and unfulfilling.

Powerless Thinking

Powerless thinking is what unhappy people use. I don't just mean unhappy because of money, *but unhappy because they think in scarcity.* Unhappy people think alike, just as happy people think alike. The same with poor or rich people. Poor people think of earning a wage, while the rich think of owning the companies and hiring people at a wage. *Likeness attracts likeness*. Birds of a feather flock together. The rich get richer and the poor get poorer, *and it is their agreements of belief that attract the experience* of being poor or the experience of being rich. It is all in the thinking!

Powerless thinking in scarcity (not being good enough) is at the core of suicide, divorce, bankruptcy, depression, drug abuse and probably all other dysfunctions. Powerless means victim and vice versa. It means anyone suffering from these horrible disharmonies don't know *who they are*; therefore, they don't feel they can attain *what they want* (victim thinking). They stop before they get to *the steps of faith and focus to manifest their desires.*

Prosperous vs. Scarcity Thinking

Economics is a way of thinking. If you want to be prosperous, choose to be around four or five prosperous friends. Soon you will be prosperous too because you will start to think of how money can work for you, rather than how you can work for money. Students from economically sound families are the ones who are getting the scholarships because they know the system of wealth. Prosperous people think in power, and they know the steps of attainment. But prosperity is really what you give rather than what you have and not just about monetary things.

Have you ever wondered why they say college graduates make more money? Well, who can afford the expensive colleges and universities? The majority of wealthy people, who think in terms of prosperity, make sure their children have access to the best tutors, teachers and opportunities. *They don't leave it up to fate. They choose their fate*. You can have that life too – you don't have to have money – you just have to think in abundance. Positive thinking is not exclusively for the affluent, but is readily available for all who chose to tap it.

◘ *Pause here and complete WORKSHEETS 7, 8, 9, & 10.*

Going for Broke

(Refer to WORKSHEETS 7, 8, 9 & 10 as you read this to see how your beliefs have created your experiences.)

Indecisive students cannot see their future. They think they cannot escape their past. This makes them feel trapped and powerless. This is just the opposite of Oprah Winfrey, Donald Trump, Bill Gates and other successful people. Do you think they wake up in the morning and say, "I wonder how things are going to go today"? Or do you think they decide how today will be? ***Obviously, they choose what they will experience by their agreements of belief and power of intentions***. Although they have very different stories, you will find they have very much the same agreements when it comes to the way they think in power. They all made an agreement with themselves that they would never feel powerless again. Thereby they choose to go after what they want. They "go for broke." It ***requires risk, courage and focused attention. They knew that whatever any human who had ever lived had achieved, they had a right to do the same and more***. This type of thinking is required for anyone who wants to think in power and prosperity. And, again, it's not just for the rich and famous. It's not what you have, it's what you think.

Stage 2: A Path to Changing Your "Should" Agreements and The Way You Think

Stage 2 is the "limbo" Stage. It's a necessary stopping point between Stage 1 and Stage 3 but is not the final destination. In Stage 2, you recognize that fear and negativity is no way to live your life. You know there has to be a better way. Your instincts tell you that a Stage 1 life is not the life you want. Stage 2 can be frustrating since you inherently know that Stage 1 is not the answer, but at the same time, you're not sure what changes to make. In this state of frustration, it is always easier to go back to what you know, back to the Stage you have been living in for years. Most people who grow to Stage 2 often fall back to Stage 1. This may happen time after time. This is the struggle between the authentic self and the expectations that have been put upon you. It is important to recognize in Stage 2 that this struggle is not something to avoid, but rather a challenge to work through to move you out of Stage 1. If you see this, you are half way there!

Waking up to this distinction is hard to do. Stage 2 is when complacency is changed into seeking intently. You have survived and coped and even mastered the techniques using all of the shallow behaviors described in Stage 1. Life becomes mundane and you are somewhat bored due to lack of adventure. You may say things like *"this is just who I am"* when dealing with adversity in a negative way. For example, devaluing or discounting a situation that didn't turn out the way you wanted.

Chances are you will need more pain to wake up and move through Stage 2. Maybe the pain will come in the form of a break up with a partner. Or maybe it will come through loss of a job or maybe an illness. *It takes pain to want to change.* Eventually, pain will lead you to seek answers to comfort your discomfort.

As you seek so you shall find. This is where you come to a cross in the road. One path has many footprints leading back and forth from Stage 1 to Stage 2. *The other path is less traveled. You don't know where it leads, but you are so tired of where you have been that you are willing to try something new.* It is scary because you can see only a few feet at a time. It requires courage and focused attention each step of the way. You are open to the unknown, open to new learning and unlearning, open to replacing your current shallow experience of living with adventure and exploration. *You are willing to review your past agreements of thought and discover why you think the way you do and how you have existed in this world that you call your life.* You want answers!

Good for you! Dissatisfaction with Stage 1 is a good thing. Wanting answers is a good thing. Finding the answers and bringing them into your everyday life is a hard thing. In order to move from Stage 2 to Stage 3 you must see and embrace what is available in Stage 3. If you can understand it, you can become it. The lessons that follow show you the path to understanding Stage 3 and the power of living in Stage 3.

LESSON 4
Embracing Creative Consciousness

*This lesson introduces the concept of **Creative Consciousness and discusses its relationship to Stage 3**. In using this term, I am referring to the higher power that creates. Each individual will give Creative Consciousness a different name based on religious or spiritual beliefs. If you don't believe in a higher power then use the term Creative Consciousness as intelligent energy. My intent is to help students recognize the creative power born within and throughout everything that exists. This section introduces some concepts which may seem less tangible and more difficult to digest than other parts of this book. Be patient and keep an open mind as you read through this section as I try at the end of this lesson to tie it together and provide you tangible advice in how to move to a life in Stage 3.*

Stage 3

Stage 3 is discovering the truth about who you are. You are as powerful as any human that has ever lived, but ***you must think from the same reference of mind as those powerful humans do***. It is discovering what you really want (your values and ideals). It is discovering the steps to create the desired outcome (faith, focused attention and action). It is co-creating in harmony with Creative Consciousness.

Stage 3 represents freedom at its highest level because you are ***no longer afraid to dream*** and go after your dreams because you know the steps of creation. You create in unity, with pure intentions of joy for all things and all people. You see in unity that we are connected to all things and people. You want in unity, seeking for others what they need. You love in unity, knowing to love others represents love for yourself. ***You look beyond the dualities of good and bad, which allows a state of peace that comes from suspended judgment***. You no longer feel uncomfortable with opposites, and instead see them as a way of contrasting differences. You have lifted the veil that hides the authentic self, reuniting you with the co-creative power within. ***This is the truth about you!***

Who Am I?

(Refer to WORKSHEET 11 to see how to create the life you want.)

What is my authentic self? This is the question undecided students must all come to before they can create the highest form of purpose and excellence and change their agreements. ***They must know who they are then they can create the life they want.*** So let's begin to define us at the highest level.

The human body is made of over **70 trillion cells**. Every organ, every limb, every sense is priceless. Yet how often during the day do we feel priceless? What makes our body's design re-manufacture itself every three to seven years? What intelligence holds the cells and atoms together? What makes us alive? It is our Spirit.

Man is the highest physical form of spiritual manifestation. It is spirit clothed in the body. Therefore, **the authentic self is spirit**. Spirit is Creative Consciousness **energy**. Likeness begets likeness. Dogs cannot beget cats. Horses cannot beget cows. Creative Consciousness begets authentic self. **Being human is the veil covering our authentic selves**. Wow! With this knowledge, we must discover how we have covered our original nakedness with a veil or a fig leaf of false agreements that **humanizes the authentic self**.

Life is Made of Beliefs, Thoughts and Perceptions

Your reality is created simply by what you think about most of the day. Norman Cousins said, *"Not even the universe, with its countless billions of galaxies, represents greater wonder or complexity than the human brain. The human brain is a mirror to infinity. There is no limit to its range, scope, or capacity for creative growth."*

In a book called *The Delfin Knowledge System* by Leslie Fielger, research shows that the brain **processes roughly 60,000 conscious thoughts each day**. Each thought transmits waves at **5,000 feet per-second from your brain to your nervous system.** Based on this scientific data, it could also mean that your **thoughts travel 5,000 feet per-second out in the universe creating your reality.** This may explain why parents are connected to children and get a **"sense"** when they need help. Or when a friend calls at just the right time because he or she has been thinking of you. **Thoughts travel in a causative and active form.** The gestation period for your thoughts to manifest depends on the energy and timing of requests you make.

The Law of Attraction

The Law of Attraction takes the principal "Like Attracts Like" (or "What You Think About Expands") and applies it to conscious desire. That is, a person's thoughts (conscious and unconscious), emotions and beliefs cause a change in the physical world that attracts positive or negative experiences that correspond to the person's thoughts. This process has been described as "you get what you think about" or "your thoughts determine your experience." Faith is a substance, matter or element of things hoped for and is a necessary element in getting what you want.

Included in the system of faith is precision focus or paying attention to what brings you harmony. ***Creative Consciousness manifests those things in our lives that we pay attention to or focus on.*** Think about it. You have used the ***law of attraction*** or this kind of precision focus before. Remember when you wanted a bicycle or a car or to go visit a place on vacation? Remember how passionate you were about getting it? Remember how you would daydream what it would be like to have it or to experience it? ***Remember how much time you spent thinking about it? "IT" was your dominate thought.*** And this is how you create! ***The dominate thoughts that are programmed into your subconscious mind are governing your life today.***

Those in harmony with their ***authentic self or Creative Consciousness*** have erased their blueprint of dysfunctional agreements. In doing so, they remove the barrier or veil of being separate from their authentic self. ***This makes them a proxy or a channel through which Creative Consciousness can be expressed. They are co-creators in purpose with all the rights and privileges to create joy and happiness.*** This was the Creative Consciousness of Christ, Mohammad, the Dahli Lama and probably all recognized spiritual and religious leaders. They had total trust in the power of faith. ***The system we use to co-create with Creative Consciousness is faith.*** This is very similar to the law of attraction which was just discussed.

Remember, we are all connected so there has to be an understanding of interdependence. Sometimes your request or desire can come immediately, and sometimes it takes days, months or years. The important thing to remember is ***if you keep thinking it and believing it, and if it is in harmony with what you think, say and do in joy, it <u>will</u> manifest itself.***

Small Steps

Like that of the tortoise, ***small steps with consistency and focus are the secret to achieving great things.*** So I say don't *think* big; it will overwhelm you. But *envision* big so you can see the direction of your journey. Then start stepping, one small step at a time. Just take today with an understanding that ***there are seasons for everything***: rest, play, work, study, giving and receiving and so forth. But we must be prepared with courage, understanding and perseverance to reach for the stars of potential.

Yet we won't have the courage to step, if we don't understand the steps of faith. Simply put: *your dominate thoughts create tomorrow*. Be conscious of subconscious thoughts because the subconscious is the magnet of attraction. What is in there will keep showing up. So if you don't like what you see in your life, you won't like the thoughts of agreement locked in the mind of your subconscious. That is why we need down time, to listen and to feel. Your feelings will show you what you are thinking. *If you don't feel free, it is because you don't think in freedom. If you don't feel powerful, it is because you don't think in power*. Once you understand this, you will walk and move and create with Creative Consciousness.

Focus. Again, pay attention with a knowledge that this is the price for whatever it is you need. Then and only then will you truly find peace of mind and rest from fear.

We Create Our Future

Carl Jung, the renowned psychologist, suggested that a man who does not believe in fate does not understand his agreements. In other words, our fate is our agreements. Therefore, we all have a crystal ball to show us our future. Our future is simply a repeat of today if we continue to think, feel and believe the same way tomorrow. A pithy phrase you may have heard is worth mentioning here: insanity means doing the same thing over and over and expecting a different result. So if undecided students have a blueprint of scarcity or of not being enough, the blueprint will continue to be the same tomorrow until a purposeful change is made.

Undecided students have the power to create the life they want. *It requires them to change their minds.* They must have faith and practice precision focus on what they want rather than what they do not have. Basically*, they must think in harmony with or aligned with the characteristics and virtues of Creative Consciousness which, at its essence, is joy*. This takes courage because they must surrender their false beliefs, blueprints and agreements. Anything of self, of ego, of scarcity, of inadequacy or of not enough creates separation from your authentic self, and must be abandoned. Living beyond scarcity beliefs and within truth unites man co-creating with Creative Consciousness on the eternal path less traveled. The unity allows undecided students to become true co-creators. They demonstrate being in harmony by seeing that we are all one spirit, one mind and one body when we take on the characteristics and virtues of Creative Consciousness. Therefore we will love our neighbors as ourselves. Not only will you live in joy, but something even more profound happens: the world becomes a better place.

When undecided students are guided to know their authentic selves, **they will never condemn themselves or others again.** This gives them the power to change their lives by changing their thinking, and great things happen. When undecided students live in harmony with their authentic selves rather than the false ones they have embraced for so long, they begin to live the lives they have always wanted but were afraid they could not have.

The Authentic Self is Powerful

The power to create exactly what you want will come through imagination. Imagination is thoughts in action. Each of our blueprints will require divine virtues if we are to reach the potential of creating a life of fulfillment, peace, joy and abundance.

The authentic self has to be the same as Creative Consciousness. Creative Consciousness is **omnipotent** (having virtually unlimited authority or influence), **omniscient** (having infinite awareness, understanding, and insight, possessed of universal or complete knowledge) and **omnipresent** (present in all places at all times). This is what we tap into when we are in harmony with authentic self.

Together as a whole, in a state of **interdependence** we can move mountains and live in peace. This is the path to harmony with Creative Consciousness. Accomplishing this would bring our earth to a vibration of glory or unity that would equal a vibration that is "out of this world."

Well, this seems like such a big task to take on! *To change the world* is an overwhelming responsibility. Or so it seems, until one realizes that **we are only responsible for changing our personal earth or life.** By changing ourselves to be in harmony with Creative Consciousness, we too will be one in purpose.

Mastering Faith is the Power of Creating

Faith is the tool of Creative Consciousness to move intelligent energy into manifestation. Faith must be mastered by each of us. In order to master it, it must be defined. "Faith is a substance of things hoped for." It is matter, or spirit or intelligent energy. **It is that of which all is made**. It is the father element on a chemistry or biology chart. And it is your *focused attention in thoughts or intention that causes faith to manifest in physical form*. If you master the tool of faith, you become master of your life. How powerful is that?

Power of Attention

The price to pay for mastering faith and creating the life you want is remarkably simple. You must pay attention! Yes, I am making this point again. If you take only one thing away from this book, let it be the lesson of paying attention – you will be amazed at what you see. It is the Law of Attraction: likeness begets likeness. A farmer knows if he plants a seed of grain, he will grow grain. He also knows if he plants a poisonous seed, it will grow a poisonous plant. It is the same with us. What we put into our brain in agreements of thoughts, beliefs and perceptions will be manifest by what we pay attention to, whether it be good or bad. Once we understand this, *we will police our thoughts embracing those that we know will create the life we want.*

Power of Thoughts

You see, we have a crystal ball in each of us. It is our thoughts. Our agreement of thought dictates our future. So if we say *I am* stupid, inadequate, a victim, or any other dysfunction, then faith by the power of attention will bring the manifestation of those dysfunctions. Why would you want to create a world of hell when all you have to do is use faith by affirming in a focused gestation period that *I am* abundant, whole, complete, unlimited, and joyful thereby creating a world that is heavenly?

The problem is most of us has at least 18+ years of victim programming, and it will take time to reverse the blueprints of agreement that have been harnessed in the subconscious mind. And *what has entered the subconscious has entered by repetitive and dominate thoughts which is faith, and faith moves intelligent energy into manifestation causing manifestation of that thought*. That is why we must pay attention to what we are thinking on a regular basis. And if you don't know what you are thinking, take a close look at your life. *Your present condition is a manifestation of your previous dominate thoughts. You have the power to determine your dominate thoughts; therefore, you have the power to create the life you want.*

Dualities of Right and Wrong

It is important to recognize that dualities of good and bad or dualities of right and wrong is the only perception that causes you fear. It is also important to see beyond dualities and judging yourself. Rather, try to see dualities as a simple contrast for understanding and building awareness.

Being at one with dualities is a consciousness principle, so you will have to come in line. The concept of the "Lion and the Lamb" comes to mind when bridging dualities. The Lion represents virtues of courage, strength and power. The Lamb represents gentleness, trust and understanding. At first glance, you may conclude that the Lion and the Lamb represent duality because they are so different. This naturally leads to thinking "should I be the Lion or the Lamb?" The answer is "be both." This is balance or harmony with self and others. This is the Yin and Yang, male and female. It will require you to see beyond dualities and therefore will require you to stop judging them. *Bhagavad Gita* sums it up this way: ***"That devotee who looks upon friend and foe with equal regard, who is not buoyed up by praise nor cast down by blame, alike in heat and cold, pleasure and pain, free from selfish attachments, the same in honor and dishonor, quiet, ever full, in harmony everywhere, firm in faith–such a one is dear to me."***

Yoga Vasishtha put it this way. ***"Since the seed does not contain anything other than the seed, even the flowers and the fruits are of the same nature as the seed: the substance of the seed is the substance of subsequent effects, too. Even so, the homogenous mass of cosmic consciousness does not give rise to anything other than what it is in essence. When this truth is realized, duality ceases."***

Lesson 6 applies these concepts to the reality of choosing a major and a career path. Hopefully you can see that by tapping your Creative Consciousness you will uncover your authentic self and authentic wants, which naturally move you away from a life of fear and indecision. In this state, all choices flow easier. You will know who you are, what you want and how to get there. This understanding is essential to choosing a major and career path.

LESSON 5
Joy Requires Truth

Extreme Thinking Restricts Joy

As discussed in Lesson 1, undecided students tend to lock themselves into a way of thinking that translates to "playing it safe." This limited thinking restricts the truth. As an example, if a student in school thinks he knows the best way or the only way to do an assignment, that student will be limited to that experience. The student doesn't know, and will not know, that approaching the assignment from an entirely different methodology could be a more joyful paradigm with a better outcome.

Students with this type of thinking will never be able to find a better way of living because they believe they have the only way. There are religions and sciences that believe the same way. Once the concept of absolute truth is conceived by individuals, their minds become closed. They will not be open to other concepts, perceptions or truths that could bring them more freedom, peace and joy.

Absolute Truth Separates Us

Absolute truth is the concept that there is *only one way* or that there is *only my truth*. Absolute truth always separates us from being united with everything or everyone outside of that belief system. Therefore it is a false concept because it separates us rather than unites us. Can you help someone who already knows it all? No, you can't. Unfortunately, the motivation for change in the life of someone with a closed mind comes in the form of pain. Eventually, they will have to become open to a new or better way or suffer in a life of sorrow and strife. So pain in your life is telling you that you haven't found the truth to set you free!

The Truth is Life Wants to Bring us Joy

Simply put, to live in constant joy we must live in constant truth. We must see, feel and think in a state of awareness beyond the world of dualities that divide us rather than unite us. That state of awareness Bhagavah Gita referred to earlier. So how do we do this? How can we live in a perfect or unconditional state of love? Let's look at the possibilities.

The word "perfect" can only exist in one of two states or conditions: a state of unconditional (*no condition therefore no duality*) <u>or</u> in the absolute condition (where there is only *one* right way or answer). The only way you can create a state of *no duality* is to have no judgment of the contrast of opposites yet still be aware of them. Perhaps this could be the "last judgment." However, judging duality is the only game in town or in the world for that matter. Every news station, every politician, every advertisement is intent on convincing your minds that you are good or bad depending on how well you live up to rules and standards. Yet you never can because the rules and standards change depending on who is talking or who is in power or what country, state, town in which you live. Therefore there can be no absolute that all limited minds can agree upon.

So how do we live in the world of duality and not be of it? This is where discernment or right-minded judgment comes into play. Discernment is listening through your inner ear to Creative Consciousness. This requires you to quiet the negative judgments going on in your mind. When you are in harmony with this Consciousness, you are beyond judging beliefs of duality and realize that this is where ***the truth about you is found.*** Then knowledge of your true essence is recognized. This truth will bring you to joy because you are the essence of perfect and unconditional love. When you tap into Creative Consciousness, you realize your destiny is joy.

Once you discover joy in your own life, you will see the stardust energy twinkle in the eyes of everyone, even those that have done terrible things. You will have glimpses of divinity in all things. You will recognize all things were created in Creative Consciousness. This new awareness will require you to turn within and listen to the echo of the real teacher. As you quiet your mind from thoughts of fear, anger, bitterness and resentment, you can begin to hear, feel and sense love, peace and joy – ultimately uniting you with Creative Consciousness, the most powerful force in the universe, to co-create.

With this concept alone you now can move past your guilt, your shame and your feelings of inadequacies and forgive your false concepts of being separate from one another because now you can see that you are created in ***intelligent energy that is only Love***. Knowing this, you could never criticize yourself or anyone else ever again. Doing so would keep you locked into the world of duality and separation.

If you haven't noticed by now, every experience you have had, has served you in developing characteristics that fall under the umbrella of Love. If you haven't come to this conclusion there is a chance that you haven't learned the lesson yet. The lesson is for us to live in love and to recognize that anything outside of perfect or unconditional love is the illusion that keeps us in conflict and separated from one another. Loving your enemy is hard to do for the proud, the right, the perfectionist and the egocentric. These behaviors protect the false self. The authentic self is not threatened by the storms that come from the world of illusions and duality. Illusions that claim your energy by protecting the false self always deplete your peace. Isn't it time you acknowledge your authentic self and come to live in joy and love?

This Chinese proverb illustrates the benefit of eliminating duality judgment.

Bad Luck? Good Luck? Who knows!

There is a Chinese story of a farmer who used an old horse to till his fields. One day the horse escaped into the hills and when the farmer's neighbors sympathized with the old man over his bad luck, the farmer replied, "Bad luck? Good luck? Who knows!" A week later the horse returned with a herd of horses from the hills and this time the neighbors congratulated the farmer on his good luck. His reply was, "Good luck? Bad luck? Who knows!"

Then when the farmer's son was attempting to tame one of the wild horses, he fell off its back and broke his leg. Everyone thought this was very bad luck. Not the farmer, whose reaction was, "Bad luck? Good luck? Who knows!"

Some weeks later the army marched into the village and conscripted every able-bodied youth they found there. When they saw the farmer's son with his broken leg, they let him off. The villagers thought this was such good luck. "Good luck. Bad luck. Who knows!" answered the farmer.

And so it goes …   Author Unknown

Much like this story, when we suspend judgment, duality ceases. Then as we watch life play out, we find everything has really been working for our good. Every difficulty was actually an opportunity for us to grow, for us to become stronger and for us to be open to new possibilities. And as we look beyond the belief of dualities, perhaps we will find the peaceful, restful state of joy we for which we have been searching. This is precisely what I mean when I say "It's All Good."

Key virtues of joy that harmonize with authentic self will need to be reintroduced in the quiet **stillness of a meditative state**. This is where we first reconnect. Once connected into this peaceful state, we will feel a sense of being at home. In communion with Creative Consciousness connected by intelligent energy, we can use more of the other 90% percent of the brain or mind that we have forgotten about. If we will listen, that peaceable light will penetrate our consciousness. We will be able to recognize with all of our senses that we are divine. And as we tap into this source, we become in harmony with joy, which is being your powerful authentic self.

True Gifts

Generosity is a true gift, and it's up to you to take the initiative in gaining this gift. Generosity is living in abundance. Some may think it means to give to everyone, but you should never give what you can't afford. You must give to self and fill your own cup full so that your giving won't focus your mind on lack or scarcity. We have all heard people say, "He would give you the shirt off his back." That is fine if he has another shirt, but to give where it causes *not enough* only leads to panic. Sometimes when we give what we don't have, we will find it really isn't a gift anyway but probably a gesture to get approval. **A true gift will never require recognition**. A true gift is free from attachments. And when we are living in abundance and are conscious of who we are, a natural flow of generosity will spring from within us. And the greatest gift is of self. Some may call this gift service, and even though we give this gift to others, the real gift is to ourselves. By giving it away, it comes back even more to us. This is the kind of life where we live and co-create in harmony or joy. Feeling uplifted, feeling joy, feeling like life gives us energy instead of draining it. It is our calling from our highest potential, but it could take time and courage to discover the form within us.

LESSON 6
Applying Concepts to Reality:
Choosing a Career Path

Career Path Connection

An undecided student may ask how the Creative Consciousness and other concepts discussed in Lessons 4 and 5 pertain to choosing a major or a career path. Well, they have everything to do with it. In fact Creative Consciousness has everything to do with every aspect of your life, not just your major or career path. First of all, students who are undecided about a major are still locked in Stage 1. ***They continue to feel their self worth, self expression and free will is dependent upon parents and other authority figures approving of their choices. In this state, they act based on what others think versus what they think. This leads to a cycle of frustration that is hard to break.***

Unfortunately, some undecided students never step out of Stage 1 during their lifetimes. These students are destined to be technicians, laborers, lower white collar management or government workers with ***someone always telling them what to do.*** Some of these are "A" students who are careful to select the teachers and classes that may not challenge them, but they are confident they will get the "A" grade. Some may earn Masters and Doctorate degrees thinking they will be safe by the amount of education they have. ***However, if they base their safety on being approved of, on materialism or on self-aggrandizement, which are all fear based, their achievements will be shallow at best. And remember, none of these paths are inherently wrong, it's simply that they likely are choosing to be safe.***

Choosing a career is like choosing a partner (refer to Lesson 7 on Personal Relationships). ***Often, the partner we choose will limit us in one form or another or encourage us to fly.*** Therefore, one should be very conscious of his partner's agreements of belief. The same is true in choosing a major. What agreements define you will also limit you or set you free. As you look at the complexity of the rain forest, the atmosphere, the glaciers or the ocean, one could conclude that there is no conclusion or limit to what one may experience. ***One could also conclude that obstacles, challenges and conflicts give us purpose and often define us when we overcome the difficulty.***

There are really only two careers in the world. They are Sales or Service. The undecided student will generally pick **service** as a career path because one of their biggest difficulties is interpersonal communication, as previously discussed. To reiterate, they don't want to say anything to look foolish or to offend anyone. Remember, they always want to feel safe. Many of these students choose careers that deal with children. Usually not conscious to the reason, they are choosing these careers to be safe. They have more knowledge than children, they are larger than children, and they have more experience than children; therefore, they can always be right, which means safety to them. Since they always have an administrator to tell them how to act and policies for them to follow, they rarely have to think for themselves. Does this sound like Stage 1? Again, a career in service is not inherently wrong – indeed it can be virtuous; however, it must be chosen by you as opposed to being forced upon you out of fear.

Many who choose computer science as a major often do the same thing. Often being a passive communicator, or passive aggressive, they will want to hide behind the safety of a computer. There are other career fields that adults go into for the same reason: safety. They enter jobs that don't allow for a lot of creativity. This adult is scared of change and rarely takes a big enough risk to make any difference. Only those who become top in their field ever get to use some of their creativity forces to manifest their highest dreams. But sadly, because of fear of failure most of these adults never leave Stage 1.

Purposeful Education

When someone experiences the difficulties of divorce, he/she becomes defined as the person who was going through a divorce. If someone has cancer, he/she becomes defined as the person who has cancer. What a limited way to be identified. Martin Luther King's difficulty was civil rights, along with many, many others. But, he threw off limited thinking. He studied the rules and agreements of the system of the world. He went through formal education and earned a PhD. He studied the Constitution. **He was focused. He had purpose for everything he did**. That purpose was about equality for his people and for everyone. His purpose came from being discriminated against. Perhaps law was the best course of study to prepare him for this endeavor, or was it philosophy, or psychology, or was it economics, history or religion? Whatever great leader you look up to will have a similar story. **The sole purpose of education was for a much larger desire than to get a good job or career. It was to improve their weaknesses, expand their minds, challenge their courage and improve their awareness of who they really are and what dreams they could fulfill if they set their minds to it.**

Education of this kind will change your thinking and your agreements of belief. Therefore, it will change your destiny. Isn't this what we are all hoping for? You must look deep inside yourself and ask "What thoughts or ideas am I weak in that hold me back in fulfilling my purpose? Am I a good communicator? Can I write about my thoughts and feelings? Do I have the research skills to gather data and statistics? Do I know how to create a business that will provide an income that will enable me to do my calling without the worry of money? Do I have the courage to try new endeavors?"

Many other questions could be asked along these lines that will direct you to the education that is best for you. ***Taking the easy classes just to graduate will mean nothing***. Accept the challenge of changing weaknesses into strengths. This will prepare you for most anything that comes your way. Preparedness is the result of walking through your difficulties and weaknesses. And ***preparedness puts you in the right place at the right time.***

Communication Skills Must Be Strengthened

Have you ever seen a poor communicator be successful? Sure it can happen, but it is rare. Therefore if students play it safe and do not overcome their fear of failure or mistakes, it will affect every part of their lives, their relationships, their schooling and their work.

Humans must communicate. Most situations/endeavors in life require communication skills. In the school setting, there is communication between student and teacher and among students. Additionally, though perhaps harder to see, every subject taught on a college campus will include communication in one form or another. Therefore it is critical that undecided students attain good communication skills with self, with others, with nature and with spirit. But before they can attain them, they will have to create new agreements of belief and shed the fears that hold them back.

Change is Painful

Most people won't seek help to change until things become very painful. ***Pain is an indicator that a person is ready to step into Stage 2*** (seeking a better way of life and wondering if it is possible). At this point, they need to find the right teacher to teach them the principles in the previous lessons and help them apply those principles to their lives. Well, it is rare to find this kind of teacher in a traditional school. Most of them are motivational speakers who inspire. One who inspires has the mark of a true educator. So look for them. They are the greatest communicators who will talk on a level you can understand. They teach the truth of who you are and what your potential is and how to attain it. They are those in Creative Consciousness, people who have thrown off the veil of separation. They represent what is inside each of you, and this is your destiny. ***To be an entrepreneur, a joyful creator of one's own destiny, a joyful creator of one's own world, a joyful creator of one's highest vibration that rejuvenates one's soul and every cell in your body is your destiny.***

Entrepreneur: The Highest Form of Consciousness and Creativity

Entrepreneurship requires risk, precision focus and attention. It is breaking free from systems that don't work. ***This is where true freedom emanates -- creating a service that will benefit mankind in a positive way***. However, in order for you to live in harmony with Creative Consciousness, greed cannot enter in your intent. If it does enter, you will mix pure with the impure and the outcome will leave you feeling empty and lacking fulfillment. Your intent must be in harmony with seeing your neighbor and mankind as yourself. And since we are of the same source of perfect love, to do harm to others is the same as doing harm to ourselves. To cheat others is to cheat ourselves. Entrepreneurship does not just happen; it requires preparation and planning.

Preparedness Calms the Storms

Often hidden in the terminology of ***preparedness is planning***. Once you have a vision of what it is you want to create, find someone who has already done it. That person will have all the steps required to get there and probably some alternative discoveries as well. Get the steps. Write them down. Plan one step at a time. Don't look past the next step once your plan is formed, or it may overwhelm you. Stay focused. Keep your vision as your dominate thought. Pay attention to doors opening to get you to the destination desired. Doing things in this order will create a feeling of safety because now you are prepared. Another way to realize what you want is to pretend you are 85 years old. Look back on your life. What do you want to be remembered by? What do you want to have accomplished? Now return to the present and start your journey.

Being Prepared Requires Faith

Being prepared is having a plan. Being prepared will require the mind to use all the principles of faith. To review:

1. *Faith is a substance of things hoped for.*

2. *There is always a gestation period for creation, but by using feelings as though you have already received the desire, your creation has to show up.*

3. *Your mind moves this invisible intelligent energy into manifestation.*

4. *Stay on track without any doubt. Doubt will cause your creation to stagnate. Doubt is not an option.*

5. *Believing is the opposite of doubt. Believing it has already manifested is the key. Then be patient with a knowledge that it will manifest at the right time and place. Take one step at a time, as you have planned, and pay the price of attention.*

6. *Decide what your day will be like. Decide how you will feel today. Decide the outcome of your difficulties. Decide to be strong. Decide to stand up. Decide to have the courage to walk through your fears by seeing the outcome.*

This is how you plan. Constant focus, believing and receiving the outcome as though it has already happened is how manifestation of your desire is achieved. It really is that simple if you will keep doubt out of your mind. Otherwise you will have to replant the seed over and over until you stay focused only on the affirmative agreement of belief. Eventually the belief will become knowledge, and your creations will become greater and greater. This is how you will create the life you want. You will be powerful beyond comprehension.

Career Path

If you still feel overwhelmed by these concepts, perhaps the following simple points will help you take the first steps in reaching a more complete understanding. Then read this book again. And again. And again!

- There is no right or wrong. It's all good!
- Freedom from fear allows you to choose a career path that brings you joy and harmony.
- Tapping your authentic self makes choosing a career much easier.
- Thinking and focusing on the career you want will make it a reality.
- Life is a journey with many forks in the road: don't be afraid to go down one, as you always have the power to change your path at anytime.

LESSON 7
Personal Relationships

<u>Maintain Your Self Respect</u>

Undecided students often struggle in personal relationships because of low self respect. This sounds harsh but it is true. They are so used to giving up what they want for the happiness of others that they find themselves in a deeper mess when they cross the line of a close relationship. Most have problems with commitment because they see it as losing more of themselves because they think they need to do what the other wants in order to be loved. This is what I mean by low self respect. The point they don't understand is that the minute they start doing what they think the other wants them to do, say what they think the other wants them to say, the attraction to one another starts to fade. That doesn't mean they shouldn't do kind things for one another or help each other. But they should never do it to be loved or to control what they want the other to do.

They need to remember to be the persons they were when they first met. This is who each of them found attractive in the first place. They weren't afraid of losing anything because they had nothing to lose. Having nothing to lose is very attractive and shows confidence. Therefore, they need to keep their friends and do things with them like before their close relationship started. If they don't, the relationship will feel like prison, and undecided students have already lived with too much restriction. They don't want more. They will have to remain true to themselves by having self respect and freedom, otherwise their relationships could be destined for difficulty and strife.

<u>Frequency is in Everything</u>

There is a frequency with every thought you think, with every food you eat, with every breath that you take, with every experience that you have, with every movie that you watch, with every book that you read and with every person that you meet. It creates a "frequency of attraction."

This "frequency of attraction" is significantly developed in your early formative years. Your experiences from birth through your early teens will show what you will attract as an adult. If authority figures treated you with love, respect and open communication then you will be attracted to people with the same conditioning. This may include a husband, wife, boss or friends. Likeness attracts likeness. But if you came from an environment where authority figures treated you with disrespect, always pointing to your faults, "my way or the highway beliefs," non-supportive or always distant, then the likelihood is you will attract a husband, wife, boss or friends who could be the same. Every interpretation of how you decided life would be, you will create it just that way. I call it a subconscious frequency that causes a chemical reaction of attraction to certain people. If your experience was negative in your youth, then your destiny could be negative until you wake up.

The way you were treated in your early years likely will be reflected in how you will be treated or treat others in your adulthood. Typically, parents who dominate create a frequency in their children to either dominate or to be dominated depending on the interpreted agreement of the child. If children experience a lot of conflict growing up, they will experience a lot of conflict in their relationships. Or they may choose relationships that will allow them to always be in control and always be right. If you don't wake up to this truth, you will run from one relationship, job or friendship after another. *Remember your present day experience is caused by your past agreements and interpretations of life.* This is why a review of your past is necessary to find the negative or false beliefs of agreement. Then you can change every negative to a positive agreement, and set yourself free by creating a new frequency that promotes peace, harmony, acceptance, understanding, gentleness, trust, love and any other virtue you would like to attract in your life.

Unfinished Business of the Past

If you feel that you love someone but also hate them too, look and see what authority figure you felt the same way about. You will find that by doing this you will have unfinished business with your past. And until you deal with the unfinished agreement that was created in your past, it will keep showing up until you deal with it. To deal with it, you need to change your past agreements. You have the power to change your agreements so that they work for you in a new positive agreement of belief which will be developed through affirmations.

Love can be blind because people can't see that they are going to recreate their past if they haven't worked through all of their negative agreements. Just know that nobody completes you except you. Two halves don't make a whole in relationships. And if you don't do your work now on negative or false agreements, you will have to do it some other time. It is the law of life. So why not do it why you are young and single. Use your current relationships to understand your past agreements. Fix them, heal them, forgive them and then move on to the new you, attracting on a positive frequency, creating a life of celebration. Do the work now! If you do, you will find your personal relationships satisfying, loving and full of joy – and even supportive and helpful in your career path. Yes, It's All Good.

WORKSHEETS 1-12

Now, let's review the practical applications of these concepts in this WORKSHEET section of this book. Remember that after completing these worksheets, reread the Lessons in this book. As you work through these worksheets, keep in mind the concepts discussed in the Lessons in this book. Some are distilled below for ease of reference. When completing the worksheets, know that there are no "right" or "wrong" answers. It's all good! The important thing is to answer as truthfully as you can, without overanalyzing it. Follow your gut (and heart) when working through these worksheets. You might surprise yourself, but I guarantee you will learn a lot about yourself and it is through this process and applying the concepts in this book to your own life that you can move to a more fulfilling life, including easing the process of choosing a career path that fits your authentic self.

- *Every expectation creates a fear or worry, of failure, of making a mistake or not measuring up.*
- *The percentage of time that you spend thinking about your expectations, your fears, your wants or your difficulties will dictate your experience.*
- *Your childhood experiences caused you to think a certain way which developed into beliefs.*
- *Your beliefs as an adult create thoughts that attract what you experience today.*
- *Separation, isolation and loneliness are the outcomes of being out of harmony with your authentic self. This started when conflicts in your life caused you to feel it wasn't safe to be you. It caused you to play it safe and try to please everyone. The only problem in doing so is that you lost your authentic self.*
- *It will take courage to remake yourself into thinking in a new way, with new results, creating a new perspective leading you back to your authentic life.*
- *You are creative, therefore creator, therefore more powerful than you can possibly imagine.*

The next worksheets are intended to reveal what percentage of time you are focusing on positive or negative thoughts, what you believe, and how to change your experience by changing your thoughts by writing a new blueprint or script that you must read daily until it becomes a reality.

WORKSHEET 1
List of Shoulds

Here is a list of expectations many students believe they should accomplish. Which of these pertain to you?

1. I should finish college.
2. I should get a good job.
3. I should make a lot of money.
4. I should marry the right person.
5. I should get A's in school.
6. I should make sure Mom and Dad are pleased with me.
7. I should keep my room clean.
8. I should keep up on my car payments.
9. I should eat healthy foods.
10. I should work out every day.

Now add 5 or 10 more things you believe you should do.
11.
12.
13.
14.
15.
16.
17.
18.
19.
20.

What percentage of your expectations do you live up to? _____%

How do you feel when you don't live up to your expectations?

WORKSHEET 2
List of Fears

Here are some things students frequently list as fears or worries. Which of these pertain to you?

1. Completing school
2. Finding a good career or job
3. Being poor
4. Not finding the right person to marry
5. Failing a class or school
6. Not measuring up or pleasing Mom and Dad
7. Not keeping my room clean
8. Not making my car payment this month
9. Not being able to afford healthy food
10. Not having time to work out every day

Now add 5 or 10 more things you fear or worry about.

11.
12.
13.
14.
15.
16.
17.
18.
19.
20.

What percentage of time in a day do you spend thinking about your fears or worries? _____%

Take a moment and compare your fears and worries worksheet to your expectations (Worksheet 1). Can you see that some of your worries come from the fear of not living up to your expectations? Can you see that really the only fear you have is that of failure, mistakes, or of not measuring up to your expectations? And can you see when you don't live up to them you feel **separation, isolation, and loneliness**? *Basically you feel* **not good enough**. *This is what I call living in the fallen state, and living in the fallen state is what I call* **Life's Only Temptation**. *When you live in this fallen state you inevitably will settle, quit or give up.*

WORKSHEET 3
List of Wants

What do you really want to experience the most in life without limitations? Do these wants apply to you?

1. Freedom to travel the world
2. Exploration of other cultures and lifestyles
3. Have fun and healthy relationships
4. Flexibility to have time to enjoy life
5. Family and friends to be happy
6. Ride my horse twice a week
7. Go for a walk in nature each week
8. Go to an event with friends
9. Meet someone new each week
10. Go camping with friends and family

Now add 5 or 10 more things you want to experience.

11.
12.
13.
14.
15.
16.
17.
18.
19.
20.

What percentage of time in a day do you spend doing what you want? _____%

Take a moment and compare your list of expectations with your want list. How many expectations are on your want list? ____

Why do you feel or believe that you must do things that you really don't want to do?

_____

_____

_____

_____

Do you see that should and expectations don't line up very well with your wants. Do you see how this creates doubt, conflict and fear?

WORKSHEET 4
List of Difficulties

What have been the biggest difficulties or struggles in your life?

1. Health
2. Divorce
3. Interpersonal communications
4. Relationships

Now you finish the list with a few more.

5.
6.
7.
8.

What values came from your life difficulties and struggles?

1. Health
2. Unity
3. Good communication
4. Healthy relationships

Now you finish what values you have because of your struggles in life.

5.
6.
7.
8.

What new beliefs of fear do you have because of your difficulties and struggles in life?

_____

_____

_____

_____

What percentage of time in a day do you spend thinking about your difficulties and struggles?
_____%

Can you see how your difficulties and struggles have served you to attain values and virtues that you may not have otherwise considered?

WORKSHEET 5
List of Frustrations

What have been your biggest frustrations you have encountered recently?

1. My weight
2. My roommates/spouse
3. My boss/job
4. My teachers

Now you finish the list with a few more.

5.
6.
7.
8.

What percentage of time in a day do you spend thinking about your frustrations? _____%

When you spend time thinking about your frustrations, what effect does it have on how you feel?

_____

_____

_____

_____

Think about anyone in your life whom frustrates you. A roommate, a friend, a co-worker, a partner, yourself; you decide. Then write a paragraph describing positive characteristics about that person.

_____

_____

_____

_____

Now how do you feel once you have identified the positive in them?

_____

_____

_____

WORKSHEET 6
Gratitude List

Name the things you are most grateful for.

1. My health
2. My family/spouse/friends
3. My eyes
4. My faith

Now you finish the list with a few more.

5.
6.
7.
8.

Put a price on each thing on your list. Hopefully, you will find it difficult to assign a value. At this moment, you may recognize that it is you that is priceless. How does this make you feel?

_____

_____

_____

_____

What percentage of time in a day do you spend thinking about the things for which you are grateful?
_____%

Review your worksheets and notice how much time you spend each day on positive vs. negative thinking. Write those percentages.

Negative _____%
Positive _____%

Based on your percentages, can you predict your future life and experiences?

_____

_____

_____

_____

Do you see how flawed it is to think the same way day after day and expect different results?

WORKSHEET 7
List of Memories

Write a one-line-per-year autobiography of the memories of events in your life, positive, negative or neutral. What happened even a year before you were born? Did any family members die, have health problems, experience divorce etc.

[Year Before Born]
1.
2.
3.
4.
5.
6.
7.
8.
9.
10.
11.
12.
13.
14.
15.
16.
17.
18.
19
20.
21.
22.
23.
24.
25.

The first 25 years will be enough for you to see where your agreements of thoughts and beliefs came from. You can write more years if you had major events in later years.

WORKSHEET 8
Beliefs Spring from Memories

Now write a belief that came from each event. For example, at age 6 Mom and Dad divorced. My belief is that love doesn't last or that loved ones always leave.

1.
2.
3.
4.
5.
6.
7.
8.
9.
10.
11.
12.
13.
14.
15.
16.
17.
18.
19.
20.
21.
22.
23.
24.
25.

WORKSHEET 9
Thoughts & Beliefs

This worksheet is to help you organize and see precisely what you really think about and what you really believe in. I suggest keeping a Journal and taking 5 minutes a night and write down your random thoughts. For example, one of my students wrote:

School is so hard!
I am taking communications class for no reason.
I need to get an appointment with a guidance counselor.
I still need to go to the fitness center tonight.
Why does Katie leave her purse and books all over the apartment?
I am so cold. Why is it that Katrina always has the air conditioner on like 63 degrees?
Am I behind in classes?
I still need to do math.
Why is everything so much money?
Why am I always eating?
I have so much to do tonight before I can even think about going to bed.
I am not going to communications class tomorrow.
I need to pick up one more class for the semester.
Did I call my mom back?
Why do my friends back home care so much about what I am doing here?
Why can't I ever get away from that drama?
Why can't they get their own lives?
I am going to get started on my homework.

Notice what thoughts have dominated her mind. What thoughts have dominated your mind? What are the beliefs behind her thinking? What are the beliefs behind your thinking?

Look at WORKSHEET 1 - Expectations. What do you believe if you don't live up to them?

1. I believe I am stupid because I got a C on my math test.
2. I believe I am bad because I had to ask Dad for money.
3. I believe I am less because I don't have a boyfriend.

Now add to the list.

4.
5.
6.
7.
8.
9.
10.

What are your beliefs when you review your fear list?

1. I believe finishing school will determine my worth.
2. I believe if I don't find the right person to marry I can't be happy.

Now finish the list.

3.
4.
5.
6.
7.
8.
9.
10.

What are your beliefs when you review your want list?

1. I believe I won't find the time or money to travel the world.
2. I believe exploring other cultures is only a dream.
3. I believe it will be impossible to have fun and healthy relationships

Now finish the list.
4.
5.
6.
7.
8.
9.
10.

WORKSHEET 10
The Cycle of Life Circle

The Cycle of Life is a Circle. The truth is that you are creative. In fact, you are the creator of your life. This means that whatever you believe or conclude to be true, is your truth. Your experiences from childhood created thoughts of conclusions I call beliefs of agreements. Your beliefs, in turn, create thoughts that attract like experiences. The cycle goes around and around until you wake up to the truth that your beliefs are the cause of your thoughts that create your experiences. **Now that's the truth!** For example, when I was 12 years old I went to an amusement park. There was a boat that would give you a ride around the lagoon. Each time the boat would take the same exact path. When I asked the conductor why he didn't go in a different direction or path he said he couldn't because the tracks underneath the boat restricted it. We are all the same as this boat according to the tracks of belief in the subconscious mind. Therefore, we must drain the lake so we can see our hidden beliefs that are governing our experiences. If we can change our beliefs, we can change the track our lives are on. This worksheet is an attempt to illustrate this point to you. And, remember, you already have the power to change your beliefs.

Now review your beliefs from WORKSHEET 8. Track your belief to your thoughts to your experience. Now you may start to get a big picture and see how your beliefs are serving you or not serving you. Know that you can create a new track by changing your beliefs. For example, let's look how one experience caused a belief that will keep you alone, separated or isolated:

Experience	<<===========➤	Parents Divorce
Thought	<<===========➤	Loved Ones Always Leave
Belief	<<===========➤	This Will Happen To Me
Your Experience	<<===========➤	Failed Relations

AND AROUND AND AROUND IT GOES!

Now, look at the <u>same</u> experience and see how changing your thoughts and therefore your beliefs will change your life experience:

Experience	<<============➔	Parents Divorce
Thought	<<============➔	An Action They Chose
Belief	<<============➔	I Choose A Different Path
Your Experience	<<============➔	Fulfilling Relationships

Go through a similar analysis on your past experiences and what thoughts and beliefs they have created and what you think, then, will be your own life experience. Now change your thoughts and beliefs and see how your life experiences can change! Worksheet 11 discusses this further.

WORKSHEET 11
Creating a New Cycle of Life

Creating a NEW Cycle of Life Circle will require a new birth of beliefs that will create new thoughts attracting new experiences. It is kind of like being born into a new life without having to physically die. You are creative; therefore, you are the creator. You are the artist of this life co-creating with magnificent powers. It will take a minimum of 30 days to impregnate your subconscious mind with the new life you want. Then you must review your new beliefs on a regular basis until they manifest into your life. So let's get started.

Write your new script describing your ideal job, your ideal relationship and your ideal experiences. If you can't see your future ideals, pretend you are 85 or 90 years old. Look back on your life. What do you want to be remembered for, accomplished etc? This will help. **Remember writing a script and reading it daily is the path to your new destiny. Your script must become scripture in order to manifest.** *Worksheet 12 provides more detail on how to write your scripts. Review the list of values at the end of this worksheet. Highlight the values that are in your script. Now write down your top 10 values.*

1. Freedom
2. Exploration
3. Flexibility

Now finish the list.

4.
5.
6.
7.
8.
9.
10.

Now write your values as beliefs from WORKSHEET 10.

1. I am Freedom therefore I experience free will and choose freely.
2. I am Exploration therefore I experience new adventures.
3. I am Flexibility therefore I am okay with change.

Now finish the list. Be specific.

4.

5.

6.

7.

8.

9.

10.

Circle the words from the list on the next page that best represents the values, qualities and virtues in your writing. Doing this will help you see clearly what you want which will make your decisions easier. If your choices do not align themselves with your ideals and values, they likely are choices that will not bring you joy.

Acceptance	Discipline	Integrity	Power
Adventure	Discipline	Intelligence	Prosperity
Appearance	Empowerment	Intimacy	Pure Intentions
Appreciation	Excellence	Intuition	Purpose
Balance	Faith	Joy	Recognition
Beauty	Flexibility	Justice	Respect
Caring	Forgiveness	Kindness	Responsibility
Charity	Freedom	Knowledge	Right-Minded
Cheerful	Friendship	Leadership	Sacrifice
Clarity	Gentleness	Love	Service
Commitment	Grace	Loyalty	Spontaneity
Communication	Gratitude	Maturity	Strength
Compassion	Growth	Moderation	Support
Cooperation	Harmony	Open-Minded	Tolerance
Confidence	Healing	Optimistic	Trust
Courage	Health	Passion	Truth
Creativity	Honesty	Patience	Understanding
Determination	Honor	Peace	Unity
Devotion	Hope	Perseverance	Wisdom
Diligence	Humanatarian	Positive Thoughts	Wonder

WORKSHEET 12
Writing Your Script/Autobiography

The final worksheet focuses on writing a script. In order to create exactly what you want, you really need to write a detailed script. The details need to be in sync with your highest potential and destiny. Read the script out loud for at least 30 days several times a day. Review the script weekly until the desire is manifested. This is the process of how you have created everything that is currently in your life whether it serves you well or not. The same process will work to create the life you want.

This worksheet likely will be hardest for you to complete, but it also holds the most reward. This worksheet contains more detail on the concept of "scriptwriting." You have gotten this far. It is now time to take the lessons you have learned, the exercises you have completed and the self-reflecting you have done and move to a prospective, action-oriented script, which is your future autobiography.

CREATE YOUR FUTURE
How do I write a script or future autobiography?

A future autobiography is really a road map of dominate thoughts to help create your destiny. With the understanding that you have now, you can write your destiny focusing on experiences on the road to your destination. Don't just focus on the destination or you may miss the trip. Why would you want to do that? Experience and discovery is the dance! So go ahead, write a future script about the dance. And you know that dancing is expressive, so "be."

1. Write down all of your abstract ideals. For example, peace, harmony, balance, freedom, happiness, acceptance. (Refer to the list on the previous page). All ideals are a derivative of Love.

2. Look at a five, ten and fifteen year marks. Write down experiences that you would like to experience physically, mentally, emotionally and spiritually within each time span.

3. It will be important to be flexible to crossroads that offer you the same ideal through experiences different from the ones you write. We don't want to create expectations. We want to create creative ways to express you with people, places, things, animals and nature.

4. If you have difficulties looking ahead, pretend you are very old looking back. See what you would like to have experienced, shared and accomplished.

5. Sometimes writing your own obituary will give you insight to what you want to experience in your life.

6. Turn it into a play. You are the Producer. You must see it clearly in order to put the Creative Director (subconscious) in motion. As you give it constant thought, it becomes a part of you, and the Creative Director will attract the experiences or Actors into your life that will harmonize with your ideals. This is the law of attraction and is the root of all causation. You simply need to keep the ideal thoughts your focus, using all of your self-love senses to bring the expressions into reality. It is a process that will happen in perfect order. So be patient and know that everything is working for your highest experience. Remember that your script becomes scripture if you read it out loud or listen to a recording of it daily. And scripture becomes prophesy which will be your destiny.

So, go for it! Trusting, surrendering and dancing in the flow of your most creative expression. Step out into the light and shine with the radiance of the perfect you. Maintain the understanding that you have nothing to hide. Demonstrate a child-like expression of being in the garden, running free without a care in the world, never to be deceived or imprisoned again by feeling not "good enough." Show yourself and the world that you are a child of Creative Consciousness and that your expression is of joy, health, prosperity and love because you are in full acceptance of everything about you. The truth has set you free from all of your false perceptions of belief. This can be YOUR life and will be your life if you so chose.

Remember too that writing a script is an ongoing process. It may take you many attempts and some time to get to a point that the script reflects your authentic self. It is precisely this process that leads to discoveries. These discoveries will not only hone your script but likely will lead to you creating new scripts in years to come.

Finally, realize that you can write many scripts that address different aspects of your life. For instance, try writing a separate script that focuses on a choice of major or career path. It's the same process, so don't lock-up because you might be a little more tentative in this area. Try and it will come. So relax and just start writing.

SAMPLE FUTURE AUTOBIOGRAPHY

Your general script could look like this:

"It is written that today at work is the greatest day of my life. I recognize service in all of the tasks that I do. All who I meet today bring me energy and they sense the good job that I am doing. I am flexible with myself as I am trained on new tasks. I am patient with myself every minute of every day. I embrace change and look forward to walking through experiences in a positive way. I am loved by all who I come in contact with and recognize my self worth just for being who I am. I am lucky to have this experience to break old thought patterns that don't serve me. I earn good money and am grateful for the abundance that I experience in life."

Reading this will bring you comfort and peace of mind. Anytime you need solutions to any problem, you simply write a script to fit the outcome that will bring you and others joy. Anytime you want to live a different experience, the methodology of attainment is the same process. You envision it, write a script and read it daily. Have faith that it will be so and it will be so. Believe it as though it has already happened and allow the gestation period to bring it forth as your actions also step in the direction of your desired goals. This is how you have created everything so far in your life, and this is how you will continue to create in the future.

Your detailed script could look like this (this script focuses on career path, but your scripts can fit any situation you want to tackle):

"I know that there is no such thing as wrong or right. Bad luck? Good luck? Who knows! I believe "it's all good." I also know that my indecisiveness about which major to choose is not about being wrong or right, it's simply a matter of me deciding what I want my future to hold. This creates a positive mindset that allows me to create any possibility I choose. There are no limitations. These are my dominate thoughts that I will constantly repeat to myself: There is no wrong or right. There are no limitations. It's all good.

I am a humanitarian at heart who loves and cares about people. But in being this way, I must maintain my own vision about what I want to achieve. I know that I can have both: I can help others *and* help myself.

My heart tells me I want to be a college teacher. The fears I have carried about pursuing this career have no power over me anymore. I can create this reality. I have a grand vision but I will also think in small steps. First, I will choose to major in English, as I love writing and both the written and spoken word. I will tell my advisor of my decision tomorrow.

I will seek out and make connections with college teachers who can help me walk down the good path. I will listen to them, but in the end, I will follow my own path. I will apply and be accepted to graduate school and work to get my Masters of Education. I will enjoy the educational process, the teachers and my fellow students.

Within 5 years I will be teaching at a small college that features small classes and lots of interaction with students. This career path will bring me joy and happiness. Where there is joy and happiness, there is no fear. Where there is no fear, there are no limitations. I know I can do this, one step at a time. Each day I will take a step in living out my script, and like the tortoise, I will eventually reach my destination, while very much enjoying the journey.

Even as I read this, my heart is filled with joy. The simple act of reading this each day brings me closer to making this script my autobiography. And no matter what happens, I always know that "it's all good."

www.ingramcontent.com/pod-product-compliance
Lightning Source LLC
Chambersburg PA
CBHW080526110426
42742CB00017B/3252